I'm a
Superhero

First Edition
09 08 07 06 05   5 4 3 2 1

Published by
Gibbs Smith, Publisher
P.O. Box 667
Layton, Utah 84041

Orders: 1.800.748.5439
www.gibbs-smith.com

Designed by Long Term Creative Group
Printed and bound in Korea

Library of Congress Control Number

2005928960

I'm a Superhero

Written by
Daxton Wilde
(and his mom)

Illustrated by
Daxton Wilde

Gibbs Smith, Publisher
Salt Lake City

Dedicated to children everywhere
who are superheroes, too.

Hi, my name is Daxton.

I am four years old,
and I have cancer.

I want
to tell you
a story
about

a
bad guy,

a
good guy,

and a
Superhero.

The bad guy's name is Cancer.

The good guy's name is Captain Chemo.

And, the Superhero is ME !

I used to throw up every day.

The doctors didn't know why I was so sick.

One day I got a big headache.

That's when they found out I had a brain tumor.

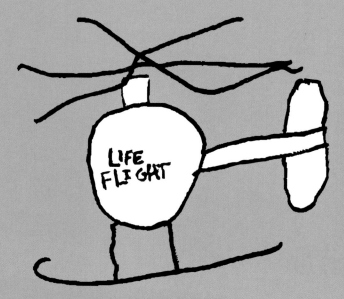

I got to fly in a helicopter. It was called Life Flight.

I thought it was a plane, but I was too sick to tell.

The doctors took my tumor out.

It was the size of a pear.

It was HUMONGOUS!

After my operation, I got real sick.
I had something they called
Cerebellar Mutism.

My mom says it doesn't happen very often.
I couldn't walk or talk; I just stayed in bed.

I got to stay in the hospital for two whole months.

I made a lot of new friends. They helped me learn to walk and talk again.

The best part about staying in the hospital was the toys!

My family
and
friends
brought me
lots of toys.
I think they
love me!

My favorite toy was a squirt gun because
I got to squirt all of my nurses.

I have a bad guy inside of me called Cancer. He makes me really sick.

I feel good on the outside, but inside of me there is a big, big fight going on.

The doctors
want to help
kill the bad
guy inside
of me, so that's when
Captain Chemo
comes to the rescue.

The doctors give me medicine. They call it
Chemotherapy, but I call it Power Juice.

A blue martian
comes to give me
my medicine.

It's not really a
martian, it's just
my nurse.

She just wears martian clothing so that
I get the Power Juice and not her.

My nurse puts Power Juice in through my power button or my Port-a-Cath.

It doesn't hurt so bad when they poke me.

I like my power button. It reminds me that I have super powers.

Another way to kill the bad guy, Cancer, is to ZAP him with radiation.

Radiation was my favorite place to go.

I made lots of friends. The ladies at the desk always said, "Hi, Daxton."

Radiation is like a cool space chamber.

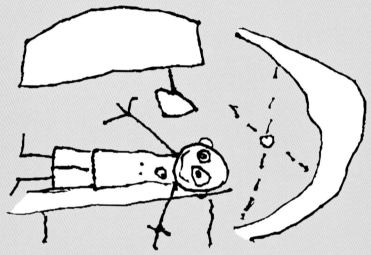

I got to lie down in it! It has red lights
and moves up and down. It makes
cool noises, too, but you have to lie really
still, or they have to start over.

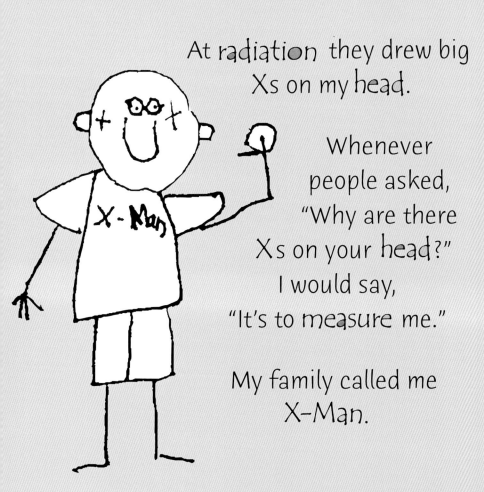

At radiation they drew big Xs on my head.

Whenever people asked, "Why are there Xs on your head?" I would say, "It's to measure me."

My family called me X-Man.

I had two best friends at radiation—
Daryn and Joan.

They were the workers who helped me
get in my space chamber. But mostly
they just played with me.

Daryn played lightsabers with me and
flew me around in my space pod.

I miss Daryn.

Joan always hugged and kissed me.
She said, "I love you, Daxton!"
I love her, too.

Radiation and Chemotherapy
made my hair fall out.

I know it will grow
back someday, but
until then, I sure
look cool!

Sometimes it is hard for me to eat, so they put a tube in my nose. It's called an NG Tube. Food goes through the tube into my tummy. It hurts when they put the tube in, but my mom and dad hold me.

It's not very fun having a tube, but I know that it makes me strong so I can fight the bad guy called Cancer.

I have to take a lot of medicine to make me feel better.

I had to learn how to swallow pills. So I practiced by swallowing Tic Tacs. It's a pretty cool trick.

Sometimes when I go places, I wear a mask. It's my superhero mask.

I wear it so germs won't get in my body. If they do, I will get very sick.

My mom says cancer isn't contagious. That means you can't get it from playing with me. It's just something that happens.

When I was in the hospital, I had lots of visitors. One day a professional soccer team came to see me.

They gave me a ball with all of their names on it. One guy even had a bald head like me!

Radiation
and
Chemotherapy
sometimes make me
feel sick, but I know
they are the good guys
that are fighting the
bad guy inside of me.

Sometimes my mom says, "It all depends on how you look at it." When I look at cancer through my special glasses, I think I look pretty cool. Cool because I get to do things not too many kids get to do. And cool because I can show everyone that I can be brave... like a Superhero.

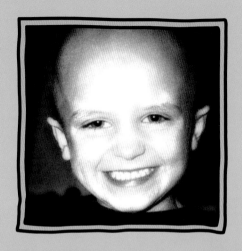

Daxton Wilde and his mom, Sherry, wrote this book to help other children battling cancer know what to expect and to inspire them to have a more positive attitude. Daxton spent much of his treatment time at home with his family where he worked on the illustrations for this book. You can learn more about Daxton by going to daxtonwilde.com.